LIGHT ON WATER

LIGHT ON WATER

Poems by

John Gearen

Antrim House
Bloomfield, Connecticut

Library of Congress Control Number: 2020948849

ISBN: 978-1-943826-75-9

First Edition, 2020

Printed & bound by BookBaby

Book design by Rennie McQuilkin

Front cover photograph © 2020 by John Gearen

Author photograph by Milton Harris

Antrim House
860.217.0023
AntrimHouseBooks@gmail.com
www.AntrimHouseBooks.com
400 Seabury Dr., #5196, Bloomfield, CT 06002

for Ann

ACKNOWLEDGMENTS

I am particularly grateful to the members of the Writers' Circle, which has met weekly for over 20 years during the winter months when my wife and I have lived in Hope Town, Bahamas, a small barrier island which often appears in these poems. The group has been open to all willing to share their work. At the end of the winter, the group has put together a performance called the Writers' Read, free to everyone on the island or the neighboring islands. We have read each year to an enthusiastic full house at the Hope Town Harbour Lodge. The Circle has been a wonderful place for writers to find their voices and to learn from other writers.

Among the members of the Circle, I am especially grateful to its organizers, Doug Hyde, Kate Oakes, Ellen McClure and my wife Ann. Doug and Ann have read and re-read this manuscript and have offered many excellent suggestions. We are all hoping that the Circle will survive after the devastation caused by Hurricane Dorian.

I am grateful also to John and Louise Bryson, who hosted Ann and me for a number of years for the Sun Valley Writers Conference, where we heard readings by W.S. Merwin and Edward Hirsch. Louise is graciously encouraging to artists of all kinds, including me and other poets who attend the conference. In addition, Ellen Bass's poetry conferences have been especially helpful.

I am grateful to my children and in-law children for their love and support, and in many cases for their suggestions on the poems in this book, and to my grandchildren for their remarkable growing up selves as well as the excellent material they have provided for poems.

My editor and publisher, Rennie McQuilkin, has been insightful and deft about all matters, from the structural to the minutely particular. He is quick to respond, encouraging and fun. I can't imagine enjoying the editorial experience more, and can't imagine a better editor.

My deepest thanks and love go to my wife Ann, not only for supporting this work and my interest in poetry, but for our life together. I am a different and better person because of her, and I feel marvelously lucky and grateful that we have shared such a joyous journey.

TABLE OF CONTENTS

III.

Begin the preparation for your death
And from the fortieth winter by that thought
Test every work of intellect or faith,
And everything that your own hands have wrought
And call those works extravagance of breath
That are not suited for such men as come
proud, open-eyed and laughing to the tomb.

from "Vacillation" by W. B. Yeats

LIGHT ON WATER

I.

Burke Women

My mother's illiterate ancestor
Yellow Mary O'Leary
of Inchigeelagh, Ireland
married James Burke,
horse trader from Skibereen,
bore six sons and three daughters, composed
"The Battle of the Pass of Keimaneigh,"
a poem still sung in Irish schools
about peasant tenant farmers with pikes
in a mountain pass, battling
landed gentry hired by the British
to enforce tithes
to the Church of England.
The farmers held the pass for days
before melting into the landscape,
anticipating reprisals to come.

Mary saw the battle.
In the poem she names some of the gentry,
curses them that they may be
"roofless, day and night,"
warns that a gallows is being built with
"the rope of vengeance twisting for their throats."

Retaliation followed
against the peasant farmers, including her sons.
All the farmers who had fought
were sentenced to be hanged.
Her oldest, John, was executed.
Two other sons went on the run.

Four generations later,
our mother, Virginia Burke,
bore six sons and three daughters,
named her oldest John.
When she sent us out into the world,
she gave us the challenge
of the Spartan mother
when sending her boy to war:
"Come back with your shield or on it."

An Irish Christmas

That first Christmas
studying in England,
I invited myself to dinner
with my distant Burke cousins
in Inchigeela, Ireland,
a tiny town in the west
near the headwaters
of the River Lee.
I knew that my grandmother's
school teacher family
had blessed her marriage
to the rough patriot
John Burke, saying
"The River Lee flows red
with the blood of the Burkes."

I met Seamus Burke on his farm
driving his sheep
down a hillside with his dog
to be "dipped" against disease
by running them through a cleansing vat
as required of sheep farmers each year.
I introduced myself
and began to tell him my story,
but to each detail Seamus said
"I know, I know," smiling
but minding his sheep
until he had to get back to work.

Their house had a dirt floor.
I was embarrassed that

they put me up at the elegant
Gougane Barra Hotel overlooking a nearby lake,
especially when my bed had feather pillows.

Christmas morning they walked me
to the house of the school teacher who,
in tribute to my distant ancestor
Yellow Mary O'Leary, the composer,
sang me all seven stanzas of the song
she still sings in Gaelic with her students
to keep alive the spirit of the revolution.

Back at the Burke house for dinner,
I was surprised they served as starters
slices of cold turkey and ham.
Strange to serve as cold appetizers
what you would later serve hot.
Only when they cleared the plates
did I realize my mistake.
They asked would I like anything else.
I asked what there was.
There were boiled potatoes and tea.

I was twenty-two.
My appetite was savage.
The potatoes were big as softballs,
simmering in a large vat,
boiled so long they were tasteless.
I ate seven.
I washed them down with weak tea.
I treasure the memories of that Christmas
but I have not eaten a potato since.

At the Track

My grandmother came from a line
of lace curtain Irish schoolteachers
in western County Cork.
She managed the affairs
of her American family,
including its investments.

It pained my mother
to see her slide into senility,
but as kids, we laughed
at her confusion
until the day she took us to the track.

I remember the horses' lathered haunches,
the jockeys' brilliant silks,
the $2 bets my sister and I placed
after polling our younger brothers,
drawing on my grandmother's $10 advance,
but most of all
I remember my grandmother,
dressed as if not just for any Sunday
but for Easter.
I'd never seen a round hat
with a lace veil,
never seen a woman instruct her grandchildren
how to read the daily racing form,
never seen her
pressed to the racetrack's rail,
lifting her lace veil
for a sharper look
as her horse thundered
across the finish line.

Quahog in Wartime

In the old wedding photo,
my mother is laughing
under a white gauze veil,
my handsome father
smiling at her.

One year later, he was stationed
at Camp Edwards, near Cape Cod.
I was born in Wareham Hospital,
named John after my grandfathers,
my father, and my mother's oldest brother,
each of these Johns the heart of his family.
They called me Quahog
after the local clam.

For the first time at age 70,
I return to their town of Cotuit,
to the cedar shake house,
the riotous rhododendrons,
the trim sailboats and grimy trawlers
wheeling on their moorings in the inlet.

My father fought in the Battle of the Bulge,
crossed the Rhine under enemy fire,
drove to victory in Prague with Patton.
My mother's brother John volunteered
for Darby's Rangers and was killed at Anzio
with nearly every man of that special troop.

My uncle John was buried at Anzio.
My father returned.

Early Mass

To beat the line
of tourists forming at 8 AM
for Notre Dame Cathedral in Montreal,
we rise for 7 o'clock Mass.

The crisp morning air
and the stillness of the small chapel
behind the main altar
cast me back to my childhood,
daily 6:30 Mass at age six.

Our next door neighbor drove me
in her humpbacked black Buick
down our gritty alley to Ascension Church,
where we knelt in the front pew
and prayed our rosaries,
her beads as big as marbles.
We heard the golden bells ring
the Sanctus, the Consecration, the Agnus Dei.
We watched towering Father Gorman
raise the communion host,
both arms extended straight up
toward the ceiling's dome.

We rode home in the gathering light, and
I was secure for a while
in my mother and father's certain faith.

Advice from Midwestern Parents

We are all God's children.

Don't look down at anyone.

Don't look up at anyone.

Look everyone straight in the eye.

God's Will

I was a war baby.
Others followed closely.

A year after my father's return
came my sister,
soon scuttling across the floor
in her dirty diapers.

Then a brother,
then six more.

After the third baby,
my mother stopped
rubbing my back
to put me to sleep.

I tried to ask her
a question once,
tugging at her skirt
for attention.
She was looking
into the middle distance
and didn't hear me.

She and my father
met me coming home

from school one day
to announce that
God had blessed us
with another child to come.
I nodded and kept walking.

I did the dishes.
I babysat.
I set about to make myself
inexpensive to be loved.

With our full family
of nine children,
my mother once left us in the house
and walked for miles in a daze
before returning.

Late in life,
she wondered
what business
had the Pope
to tell her or anyone
about birth control.

Mother and Child

As a girl,
my mother once hunted down
a boy twice her size
to pay him back
for bullying her younger brother.
When she started dating my father,
she once slapped him
for going home from a party to meet his curfew.
She said, "Tell that to your mother."
She rode and jumped horses.
She wrote a personal advice column.

She married my dad as he left for World War II.
He served five years.
I was given his name exactly,
in case he didn't return.
My face in the photos of those years
shows how happy I was to be with her.

After dinner on the night my father returned,
I told him, "It's getting late.
You'd better go home
or your mother will spank you."

My mother was Catholic.
She raised the eight more children
God gave her. My next brother remembers
when her bedtime stories stopped.
I remember her fingertips
rough as sandpaper from all the laundry.

She once said, "I love you all very much,
but don't ask me about anything that happened
in the years 1958 to 1963."

She had made so many sacrifices
that I was shocked when she picked the cashews
out of my serving of mixed nuts. I liked cashews,
so I tried to thwart her.

My mother died of cancer at an age
years younger than I am now.
I wish I had helped her find
every last cashew.

An Irish Family Raising

"Awww,"
said my aunt
when I skinned my knee raw,
her sympathy clearly fake.

The nine of us learned early
to be tough.

My mother's dad, Grampa John Burke,
made common brick in a rickety kiln.
He had started his own oldest son John
driving loads of bricks to customers at age 14.
When John once accidentally
dumped a load in a busy street,
Gramp came to reclaim it,
saying just, "Only you, John."

When I reported for my turn of summer work,
he grabbed with his mitt
one hot brick off the line,
holding it to my face.
The heat singed my eyebrows.

He told me to keep moving at work
"before the sun burns your ass."

Our hearts went underground.

Summer Jobs

My father got me summer jobs
with a construction crew.
The foreman called me "College."
Only the black laborers talked to me.
I whelbarrowed loads of wet cement,
threw shovelfuls up to the scaffold
for the Czech bricklayers,
careful not to splash their ankles.
I shoveled debris after a demolition,
avoiding all the rusty nails
in splintered strips of lathe.
I spent my last day
jackhammering the marble entrance to a bank.
Back home that day, I fell asleep face down,
missed dinner, woke eighteen hours later.

How will the grandchildren ever know
the satisfaction of a jackhammering job well done?

Ragnarok

My father grew up on daily Mass.
After Pearl Harbor, he volunteered at 26,
served the length of the War.
He led troops under fire
across the Rhine, then raced them
down the Rhine with Patton
to Prague and victory.

He couldn't keep his children
Catholic, couldn't herd us
in any one direction.
He called us Coxie's Army.

He educated all of us,
insisting on Catholic schools.
The six boys rejected his alma mater.
Soon Notre Dame and Spring Hill
gave way to Reed College
and University of Wisconsin.

We all deeply honored his military service,
but none of us went to Vietnam.
One turned twenty-six.
The others drew draft lottery numbers
high enough to avoid service.
We were all relieved to miss
a war we opposed.

To my father it must have felt
like the Norse myth Ragnarok,

where the one-eyed trickster Loki
plunges Thor, Odin,
the whole pantheon of gods
into chaos and darkness.

My father died as he lived,
like a soldier.
Each day to the end,
he went to early morning Mass,
taking Communion,
praying for us all.

Italian Pants

My father was a saint.
Everyone loved him.
(I took after my mother).

He loved our village,
sponsored its Fair Housing Ordinance,
became its President.
He shopped locally,
didn't negotiate even
the price of a new car,
saying that a man
is entitled to his profit.

He was dapper.
(I took after my mother).
He shopped for clothes
at an expensive village store
named Spaulding's.
Fine materials.
Expert salesmen.

A few years after he died,
Spaulding's went
out of business.
For one final sale
they brought back
their expert salesmen.

Attracted by the discount prices,
I stopped in.
(I took after my mother).

The salesman,
back from Wisconsin
for the event,
recognized my name,
said he'd served
my father.

I had bought two suits
when he pointed me
to a cashmere sportcoat,
a black turtleneck,
and some fine Italian pants.

I never spend money on clothes
(I took after my mother),
so when I got home,
my wife just laughed, saying
"After he mentioned
your father's name,
I guess we are lucky
you didn't buy out the store."

But I do look good
in those Italian pants.

The Grey Goose

I call my baby sister
the Grey Goose,
from the old spiritual
about a goose who is killed
by man many times,
but still magically survives.

Her breast cancer
was the size of a softball
before she went to the doctor.
Even with a stem cell transplant,
they gave her little chance.

Today, fifteen years later,
she is told she has lung cancer,
already spread.
The string of Marlboros
never stopped.
She always hated
being told what to do.

I remember her as a young girl,
lithe and brown,
making her left hand layups
in alley basketball,
before she gained weight,
stopped school,
filled her apartment
with stuff she hoped to use,

like five George Foreman
barbecue grills.

She still signs her family emails
"All my love."
She means it.
She delivers it.

The song ends:

The gun went a booloo,
Lord, Lord, Lord,
Oh, the gun went abooloo,
Lord, Lord, Lord.

She went flyin' o'er the ocean,
Lord, Lord, Lord,
With a long string of goslins,
Lord, Lord, Lord.

Last Chance

I come to visit my Grey Goose,
surrounded with oxygen tanks at home.
Her doctors have decided
she's going to the hospital
for more operations.
A few times each day
she strains to draw breath.
It comes on suddenly
and lasts for half an hour.
She consents to the operations,
saying she can't live like this.

I follow the ambulance.
I sit with her for the intake questions.
"Have you ever smoked?"
"A pack a day for 40 years
until my lung cancer was diagnosed."

They review her list of medications.
Inhalers. Heart meds.
Pills for depression. A kit for sleep apnea.

They deliver a "cardiac" dinner:
pieces of fruit with cottage cheese,
spaghetti with red sauce.

She takes one bite,
starts laboring to breathe.
The veins stand out
on her temples and forehead.

I hold her hand.
Nothing to do.
Finally, it subsides.

The doctor briefs her on the operations:
opening clogged arteries,
using "paddles" to restore the heart's rhythm.

He describes the risks.
She says only ordinary measures,
no intubation.

She tells me she is scared.
She says, "How could I have been so stupid?"
I tell her, "It doesn't matter now.
You are a wonderful person.
That's what's important."

I wonder about these efforts,
thought too risky eight weeks ago.
In the end, they all involve
the same terror of suffocation.

I try to see the positive.
In a few more months,
maybe she will see
her beloved Cubs
win the World Series.

The Faithful Chorus

My sister's oxygen level plummets
from a walk to the bathroom.
An ambulance ride to the emergency room
takes her back to intensive care
for a blood transfusion, an oxygen feed.

I help her into bed,
feeling her back, swollen with fluids.
She's gained back the fifty pounds
she lost in her last emergency stay.

"I guess it's sacrifice or die," she says.
"But Belmont Village has great shrimp scampi.
I can't resist two scoops of chocolate ice cream.
Must be my genes."

Again begins the contrapuntal chorus
of her seven faithful siblings.
"Leave her. Bind her not,"
say those wanting to let her die as she lived,
relishing scampi and chocolate.

"Doesn't she see that diet and exercise
are the only levers she has?"
say those desperate to help her live,
or at least try to live.

Released from the hospital,
she cancels on the family's Christmas party
because they took away her car.
The faithful siblings celebrate with an empty chair.

Eagle Waters Resort Once Again

for Paul and Erin Barbato

You chose
for your own good reasons
to get married here
on Eagle Lake.
What a gift it is to us
to reclaim the old resort
with its scattered cabins
under giant white pines
where we spent summer vacations
through your growing years.

I walk around the main house
and there it is,
the low wall
where each year all nine of us
lined up in age order
with all our children
for one last full family photo
before returning to Chicago
at summer's end.

Your sister's wedding toast
makes plain how deserted
you felt when your mom died so young,
how your love for your new bride
has carried you
such a long way back.

Your handfasting with her
in a ceremony at the lakefront

draws our hearts
to reclaim the place
where we stood twenty years ago
with our sister, your mother,
to be photographed together
for what we knew
was one last time.

II.

Egyptian Mummification

In Egyptian mummification,
before the body
was embalmed and wrapped,
the organs were extracted,
the lungs, the intestines,
the liver and stomach.
Even the brain was removed.
The heart alone was left in place.
In the afterlife with the gods,
all that matters is the heart.

Taxis in Cairo

Cairo distresses
my wife's soul:
the constant haggling,
the insinuated relationships,
the wild driving,
especially by taxis.

She insists
on white metered taxis,
not the ever-present unmetered
black and white jitneys
who hustle you in
but don't let you out
without a hassle
and a big overpayment.
Even the white ones
straddle lanes,
cut each other off.

So when we find a white taxi
with a well-spoken man
who drives more slowly,
she has found an oasis.

When the driver takes a call
and announces with joy
that his wife
has given birth to twins,
Miriam and Sarah,
he kisses his right hand,

first back, then front,
and raises his hands,
praying thanks to Allah.
We are both moved,
congratulating him.
My wife tells him we have a Sarah too,
and dabs at her eyes.

We arrive at our restaurant
after a long drive.
He says his meter is broken.
He charges 50 Egyptian pounds
and has only 40
in change for 100.

After the meal,
we find a white taxi back.
The ride is short.
The metered charge is 8 pounds.

We worry for Egypt.
Eighty million people,
increasing one per cent
every nine months,
the government urging
a family size of four children.
Now this new pressure:
every thirty minutes,
a new Miriam and Sarah.

Marrakesh

Once in Marrakesh,
wandering through
the central market
past the snake charmers
and the grillers of shish kebab,
I saw a man sitting alone
in the lotus position.
Only later,
when another man
came to him howling,
cradling the side of his face,
did I see on the ground
the pair of pliers.
The howling man paid.
The seated man inserted his pliers
into the howling man's mouth and jerked.
The howling man walked away satisfied.

I had not thought
again about the pliers
until my dentist
wedged my mouth open
for what he called a routine molar extraction.

No matter what instrument he used,
each piece of tooth he seized
shattered and splintered
across my tongue.
Finally, he dug into my gums,
excavated and showed me
one bleeding root.

"Now for the other root,"
he said.

It made me miss
that clean jerk in Marrakesh.

Swashbuckling

We are in Cuba,
our daughter's request
to celebrate her 30th.

Our *Lonely Planet* guidebook
recommends a restaurant
in a movie location setting,
on the top floor of a spectacularly
dilapidated Havana tenement,
which reviews describe
as "swashbuckling."

My wife is afraid:
Will the elevator make it
to the restaurant?
Will the tenement stay standing
during our meal?
What, exactly, is
swashbuckling food?
She pictures rat droppings.

Our daughter insists.

My wife says she will join us,
but she will eat
before we go.

Quebec

After my father
returned to my mother and me from the war,
the torrent of children began.
A girl, four boys and then twins:
a girl who slept by night
and a boy who slept by day.

My father asked my mother's sister
to care for her and the nurslings,
packed the older six into the green and white
Country Squire station wagon,
drove northeast through Wisconsin,
through Sioux Ste. Marie, Ottawa, Toronto,
up the St. Laurence past Montreal.
We ate fast food every meal.
I finished my younger brothers' scraps.

At last we reached Quebec,
where I bought a school tablet
from a pretty shop girl
who spoke only French,
rode in a *caliche* whose driver told us
"Is on my right is the Plains of Abraham,"
and one night when my father splurged,
tasted Vichyssoise soup.

Sixty years later,
on my next visit to Quebec,
at the end of dinner at the Café du Monde,
I am polishing off my wife's *pot de chocolat*

after finishing my *profiteroles*,
confirmed for life since age 10
as a Francophile gourmand.

My Mother in Hope Town

My mother would have loved Hope Town,
the barrier island settlement
we have found.
Nothing is available,
so everyone makes it up,
as my mother used to do.

Her father earned millions making brick
but lost it all in the Great Crash
by investing in margin stock.
The next year, as a teenager,
my mother shared one pair of stockings
with her sister,
and to make up for what couldn't be bought,
created games to entertain her younger siblings.

When I was young,
she gave me raw clay,
fired my creations in the oven.
She made me a Halloween costume so real
I was afraid to wear it home from school.
She directed her nine children
in an annual Christmas tableau,
stern with the actors,
even the ox and the ass.

In Hope Town, the respected hotel manager
makes his own go-cart,
enters it in the annual race
down the island's biggest hill.
He once crashed it,
breaking ribs,

but entered again
the next year.

In the yearly golf cart float parade
a local matron won the prize
dressed like an angel
waving her wings
from the front of the cart
like the figurehead on a ship's prow.

Hurricane Floyd struck the island
dead center.
Waves threw sand from the Atlantic beach
into and through the houses,
leaving only bare ravaged coral.

Within days after the storm,
someone begged bushels of sea oat seedlings
from the mainland.
The next Saturday,
nearly one hundred people
formed a line down the beach
with their backs to the sea,
planting sea oats in the dune,
hoping the rhizome roots
would hold the new sand
thrown up by the waves.
The photo in the island's Museum
shows the widely varying backsides
of those bent over, planting.

My mother would have loved
to beg those sea oat seedlings,
to plant them in that line.

Bahamian Golf

For Andre, Valdo and Vernon

We three Americans
join three Bahamians for golf
in the islands.
Often our teams
set nation against nation.

The Bahamians are a little older.
One threw out his shoulder
grabbing the piling
as his boat approached the dock.
Another can't grip the club firmly
for the arthritis in his hands.
But they each once played
on the Bahamian national team.

I bring my GPS sky caddie
and a bottle of water.
They bring a cooler
of Bahamian beer.

On the first tee in the US,
players announce their handicaps,
and the best player gives strokes
to each other player for the difference.
Here, the Bahamians negotiate the match
with extravagant self-deprecation
and high compliments to the opponents
about their recent play.
They always win an edge in the bet.

Once we begin,
we Americans study our shots,
curse our bad ones,
suffer over short putts.

They tease each other
with made-up childhood names,
laugh at their bad shots,
tell them to "just go in the bush,"
talk about where old friends have gone,
about growing up in Nassau
in the ice cream shops and music joints.

One of them plays in golf shoes
he hasn't used for so long
they have begun to come apart.
On the fourth hole,
the cleated soles fall off.
He leaves the soles where they fall,
finishes the round in his loafers.

Late in the round,
one hits his ball
into the impenetrable bush.
They look for it
as the talking continues.
He finds his ball and shoots it
out of the bush, the other
in the path of his shot still talking.
Across the fairway, we shake our heads.

We finish the 18th hole.
The match is close, but
they win every bet.

On the way home,
they stop and treat us
to Bahamian beer.

As we wait for our boat ride home,
one of them starts dancing,
singing the 50s Platters' song
"It's Twilight Time."
We each recall
where we first heard Elvis.

Bonefishing with a Brother

Our bonefish guide
drives us full throttle
across the shallow flats,
weaving through the mangrove outcrops.

When we stop, we are alone.
Not another boat for miles
under the wide blue sky, the rising sun.

My old arm reaches for yours,
strong as old arms go,
to steady myself up to the foredeck
to take the fly rod.

The silver fish's scales mirror
the mottled sandy bottom.
Our guide says, "First look next to the boat,
then cast your eyes away
as far as you can see clearly.
Pick up the slightest motion."

He poles the boat from his platform.
Only the thrust and suck of his pole
break the silence.

Suddenly, he calls:
"John, cast 40 feet at 10 o'clock. Then
strip, strip your line
until the fish sees the fly and strikes.
Now . . .pull the line low in a sweeping arc,

so the hook sets in its hard mouth.
Let the fish run;
bend your rod high for tension."

The fish races away
straight across the flats,
tearing blue line off the reel
down to the backing.
The fish stops.
I start to reel.
It races again,
this time to my left.
It stops. I reel.
Again and again this dance.
Finally, the fish tires.
As I reel it to the boat,
I see its shiny crescent form,
its big eye.

Then you take my arm
to mount the foredeck.
I watch you hunt and cast.

After riding back at day's end,
water now churned by a fresh wind,
we again reach arm to arm
to help each other
from boat to low dock,
soaked slippery by the slapping waves.

To a Snowy Egret

You splash on stilt legs
through muck,
stalk fish,
spear through silt,
toss and swallow.

How can your feathers
be so white?

Yeats in the Islands

Yeats recommends that we "come
proud, open-eyed and laughing to the tomb,"
and so it is on our out-island
where medical care
requires a ferry to the main island
and a flight to Florida.

Last year I sang
shoulder to shoulder with Steve,
the only other bass
in a tiny church choir.
Steve sang with joy.
He wrote and illustrated
children's books about our island,
picked flowers from neighbors' yards
which he arranged for each Sunday service.

Before the next Sunday's choir,
Steve had a stroke.
Friends ferried him
to the main island,
ministered to him on the way.
His chartered flight crossed the Gulf Stream
to a Florida hospital, but he died soon afterward.

With age comes caution.
Some sell their houses,
move to the mainland.

But others like Adelaide keep returning.
At age ninety-four she swims
every day in the cold ocean,

commanding young men passing by
to help her in and out
through the breaking waves,
proud, open-eyed, and laughing.

Rage Across the Barrier Reef

Rage boils across reefs,
jackknife of old Macheath, dear.
Sharks' teeth pearly white.

Bonefishing on Sunday

I skip the hymn-sing Sunday at Church
to bonefish with a buddy in the Marls.
The guide swerves our boat
through the shallow flats,
sea and sky the same delicate blue,
horizon marked only
by distant mangrove outcrops.
The wind barely ripples the water,
the only clouds cumulus puffs at the horizon.

The bonefish see us
as soon as we see them.
They flash away when our flies hit the water.
We learn to cast well ahead of them and wait.
We hook one who crashes back
through the mangroves to safety.
Then we hook and land one after another:
a five-pounder extracted
from its weave through the mangroves,
seven by lunch time.

Over lunch, our peanut butter sandwiches
tasting like steak, the guide sees another one,
grabs my rod and hooks a 7-pound fish.
It dives through the mangroves
but stays on the hook.
He wades to the edge of the mangroves,
finds the line where it emerges,
hand-lines the fish to himself,
insists we take pictures of him,

thrusting the fish toward us
to make it look bigger.

After lunch, still giddy with triumph,
he poles us listlessly around a new bay.
We take turns standing on the bow,
rod ready for hours,
finally catch one more fish.

A cool wind rises.
The sky is still deep blue.
He gives us a half hour warning at 3 PM.
When he quits at 3:23,
I want to hold him there,
not just for seven minutes.

We race back through the mangroves to the dock.
A cloud covers the sun for the first time.

Later, I hear about the hymn-sing at Church,
some of my favorites.
My choirmates loved it.
I would have too, but on this Sunday
it could not have compared
to the Church of the Marls.

Hope Town Vanishing

"It all goes by so quickly,"
said my grandmother,
deep in dementia.

Especially here in Hope Town,
where we watch sunsets
over the harbor
breathing in the salty west wind,
listening to the clanging in the riggings
as the sailboats swing on their moorings.

Where writers meet weekly
to share their souls,
where we are past caring
about career or money,
where friendships can be as quick and easy
as in grade school.

Where our view of the blue ocean
from the church window
is slashed by a palm branch,
where sharks cruise inside the reef
along the white sand beach
at the Hope Town Lodge.

Where an old friend
is flown out for treatment,
where a few close friends have failed this year
to make it back to climb the ladder
up from Albury's ferry to the Hope Town dock,
where more may fail next year.

Casuarina Cemetery

Once upon a time on this island,
a cemetery tucked behind a seaside ridge
grew thick with casuarina pines.

The pines dropped cones
onto the stone lids
of the standing limestone coffins,
whose raised rims held them there.
The cones sprouted roots
that pierced the coffin lids,
chewed through bones into ground.

The feathered branches
of the casuarinas grew tall,
waved and sighed in the wind,
created a peaceful, sacred place
to sit and think.

Environmentalists decreed
casuarinas were not native.
All were cut to the ground.
Now that cemetery lies
treeless and sun-bleached.

No one comes to sit and think.
No one comes at all.
No more do fecund bones
go feathering toward the sun.

My First Bonefish Guide

I met him first as he sat at the end of a bar
he called his office,
cigarette hanging,
cold sky-blue eyes.
Already, postcards in town
featured a painting of his face.
He was called Bonefish Dundee.

When he "carried" me bonefishing,
he jumped lithe and barefoot
from the dock into his old flats boat,
gear in a weathered oak bucket,
long wooden pole with two trident points
laid along the gunwale.

From his platform in the stern,
he poled us along the mangrove coastline.
He spotted bonefish in the inlets
long before I could see them.
He'd tell me where to cast, saying
"Don't yuck it, sir."
Landing one silver fish per day
was enough for me.

At his 70th birthday party,
he and his brother sat erect receiving guests,
blue eyes looking to the middle distance.
Self-sufficient from growing up
in a remote lighthouse, they were
proud of their voluminous gardens,
their prodigious fishing.

Now he sits alone in a chair on his porch,
lung cancer returned,
lithe body wasted,
hair gone to stubble,
We bring the banana bread
he used to enjoy.
He can no longer eat it.
We tell him we love him.
He says, "I love you too."
Those blue eyes flash.

Wooden House on the Ocean

Friends tell us
to leave this island, or
at least move away from the ocean.

Our wooden house
sits on a small dune
fifteen yards above the high tide line.

Hurricanes come more often.
With the ocean level rising,
they scour out beaches,
even those behind thick barrier reefs.
Some friends' houses now sit on a steep bluff.
No telling when our turn might come.

My wife jokes
we should sell the house to a Republican
who still denies climate change.

We drink our morning coffee
in our open wooden gazebo on the dune crest.
Late each afternoon
at what my wife calls "shark time,"
I dive into the surf to swim in the waves,
then backstroke the curl of a big swell
onto the shore.

At night when I can't sleep,
I press my nose
into the bedroom screen,
wet with dots of salt spray,

to smell the ocean wind,
to see Orion's belt
in a field of stars,
to watch on the distant water
the five flashes, then a pause,
made by our island lighthouse.

I'm not leaving this place
until I have to.

Returning North in Early Spring

In the islands,
the warm, wet air is fecund.
Green film forms
inside my water bottle.
Mildew creeps up
building walls.

We slice open
an overripe avocado.
Already,
roots shoot
from its seed
and eat into flesh.
Friends give us
clippings from their plants.
We shove them into our sandy soil.
The sticks sprout roots and grow.

Back north in early spring
on Lake Michigan,
the air is crisp and cold.
Whitecapped waves break
and tear at the ice
that still hugs the shore.
Northwest winds
jangle our wind chimes,
bend our Douglas firs,
even faintly move the highest branches

of the hundred-year-old oak.
No flowers yet,
matted grass still pale
on the hard ground.

The Red Oak

I wake to see through the dormer window
the sun strike flat on the rough grey bark
of the hundred-year red oak
that stands on our Michigan foredune.
The northwest wind riffles its leaves,
but does not bend even its smallest branches.

For nearly half of my life
I have watched this tree
filter the moonlight
through its bare branches in winter,
stand through fierce spring storms,
when dropping just one of its large branches
would have crushed our house to matchsticks.

The arborist warns that more bare branches
this spring just mean aging.
They must be trimmed, not now,
because oak wounds heal slowly,
leaving it vulnerable to disease,
but in the fall, when the weather turns cold.

I have loved this oak so long
I hope it outlives me.

Whitewater

For thirty-nine years
we have paddled this wild
Wisconsin whitewater river,
first in tandem canoes,
now in solo kayaks.

We have slept at a lodge
overlooking the rapids,
watching the fly fishing below.
We have paddled with a master guide,
helped her plant white pine sprigs
after a tornado crushed her buildings,
wrecked and scattered her boats,
stripped her trees to bare stalks.

Now, the lodge is up for sale.
So is the local gas station
with the hand-tied dry flies.
Even our guide says she would sell
her dream business
to the right young couple.

We are weary ourselves,
down to three paddlers:
the banker's bank has failed,
the lawyer and teacher plan retirement.

The first day, we all spill our kayaks.
Even our guide
goes to bed early.
Our final day,

she takes us
to a new stretch,
shows us the forked seven-foot falls
at the take-out point.
Last season a canoeist
took the wrong fork,
died on the rocks below.

We three look at each other,
knowing we will never
in our lifetime
be able to take that falls.

We begin the day's
six rapids, the first,
a three-foot waterfall.
We scout it with her.
She asks which route we'd take
if she weren't there.
We choose
the heart of the current,
the one that makes
the deepest "V" downstream.
"Too much water,"
she says, and
shows us another one.

We paddle single file.
We all make it.
Her camera catches
my bright blue kayak
with two feet of its nose
in midair over the falls.
Afterward she tells us,

"That was first grade."

Downstream we go,
the river gathering force.
We scout, we guess wrong,
she shows us the way.
We negotiate a long puzzle of boulders.
We plow through a monstrous wave.
Next, she takes a rapid first
to show us a nasty hydraulic
at the end of a run.
It spills even her,
but we can then see to avoid it.
Next, she chooses as a route
a ribbon of water
down a long rock face.
"Too much current everywhere else,"
she says.
We all snake down after her,
our kayak hulls scraping the rock face.
Then the river
narrows to a canyon.
We fly down the cascades of water,
sheer rock walls on either side.

We come at last
to the seven-foot falls.
She says,
as she has throughout the day,
that we should try
only if we are comfortable,
but she is confident
that each of us
can make it.

And so,
we try.

In turn, we each
float down the long entry,
gathering speed,
enter the narrow chute,
rock wall on the left,
shallow slab on the right,
shoot out toward the rock ledge
and the rooster spray of water
leaping three feet in the air
before falling to the pool below.

The banker
has his kayak turned completely
in descent, lands
staring straight back
into the maw of the falls.
The lawyer is blinded
by the rooster spray,
his strong glasses useless
as he hits the water
with his eyes shut.
The professor
almost scrapes to a stop
on the slab rock
before shimmying back
into the ribbon of current,
powering into the rooster spray,
landing upright, joyous.

We bring our kayaks to shore.
We haul them up the bank.

We thank her,
hug her,
head for home
in triumph and wonder.
Maybe there will be
a 40th year.

The Old Walnut Trees

Old walnut trees
ring the circle drive
entering our lake house.
In the fall,
their leaves are first
to yellow and drop.

Their highest branches
have begun to crack and fall.
One sheared a large limb
from our tulip tree.
Another caught
on a lower branch,
dangling awkwardly
above our garage roof.

The arborist says
the trees are healthy,
just old.
Their limbs are
light with age.

To preserve the species,
older trees make more walnuts.
In a strong wind,
the heavy harvest of walnuts
swings back and forth
until the limbs give.

Labor Day

Children and grandchildren flown home,
beachhouse empty,
crib collapsed and stored,
sheets stripped and washed.

Spent fireworks hauled up the beach stairs,
windsock rippling in the stiff breeze,
porch chair pillows taken indoors,
rain spitting through the screens.

Skylight windows closed,
wren house stored away till next spring,
hosta nibbled to stumps by deer,
ground turned hard under brown grass.

First fall fire in the stone fireplace,
last mouthfuls poured
from nearly empty wine bottles.

Now out for dinner.
Anywhere open.

Autumn Storm Over the Lake

Late in the afternoon
the storm sweeps from the west
across Lake Michigan,
blowng the windsock stiff and horizontal,
ripping clusters of leaves
from the hundred-year-old oak,
driving them to the ground.

Acorns striking the wooden deck
sound like raps at a door.
We unchain the hammock, grab it
and run for the screen porch
as the first fat raindrops
splat on our shoulders.

Drift Fly Fishing for King Salmon

For drift fly fishing,
anchor 9 feet of 12-pound monofilament
to the end of the shooting fly line
coming off your reel.
Thread that through a black snap swivel
and tie the other end to a barrel swivel.
Anchor six feet of 8-pound tippet
in the other end of the barrel swivel.
Attach to the end of the tippet
your dropper fly,
a Woolly Bugger,
a Green Butt Skunk,
or an Egg-sucking Leech.
Anchor 3 more feet of tippet.
in the eye of your dropper fly.
Attach to the very end
your salmon egg point fly.
Open the snap of your snap swivel.
Attach the weighted Slinky Drifter.
Start casting.

Stand facing across the current
so the target fish are between
12 and 2 o'clock downstream.
Cast the Slinky Drifter
ten feet upstream,
hold the rod tip high
and keep the line tight.
Feel the Drifter sink and
tap the bottom
as your rig nears the fish.

If the line pauses at any time
while your flies drift
through the strike zone,
even as briefly as if
your line touches a floating leaf,
set the hook hard.
It may be a rock,
but if not,
you have met the King.

October Turns November in Michigan

Squirrels race across the grass,
carrying in their teeth
walnuts big as their heads.
Redbreasted Nuthatches,
back from the north,
peck the suet.

The Burning Bushes
flame red,
bright gold sugar maples
are half bare,
old black walnuts
nearly leafless.

On the lakeside dune,
the basswoods' few leaves shiver.
Only beeches and red oaks
hold nearly all their leaves,
the beeches blanched yellow,
the red oaks copper,
hanging on.

My Guide Explains Crossbow Hunting for Deer

Once we get a couple of frosts,
they start rutting and moving at night.
You'll see twenty dead on the highway.
They have no predators here.

When you hunt,
you can fool their ears by being still,
you can fool their eyes with camouflage,
but you can't fool their nose.
Dead Down Wind
sells earth pucks
you put in bags with your clothes,
but nothing works.
You have to be down wind.

I shoot my crossbow twice a week,
twenty arrows.
I hate to just wound an animal.
You shoot behind their front legs,
for their heart and lungs.
From thirty yards away
my arrow goes right through a deer.
Beyond that, the arrow slows down.

My buddy and I drag them out.
I dress them myself.
You get forty pounds of meat.
The back straps are the tenderest part.
No roasts, but steak,
hamburgers, salami.
The meat is so lean we mix it with pork.

I throw the carcass in the woods
for the coyotes,
or dump it in my buddy's lake.
The bullheads eat it all.
No need to waste a thing.

The Old Wheelbarrow

Lately, I use more and more
the old wheelbarrow
I must have gotten long ago
for some single large task
at our place on Lake Michigan.

I love the barrow's rude handles,
varnish worn to raw wood,
rutted almost to splintering.
I love its fat rubber wheel,
its wide shallow belly.

Over time, I begin to wheel
all plant clippings and tree branches
to the crest of the dune
to cast them over its edge.

Soon I park the barrow
upright each night,
close to the house,
ready for morning.
I wheel my tools to each task,
chain saw, garden hose,
hand clippers,
then carry the tools back
piled on the day's last load
of branches and clippings.

Once, walking the wheelbarrow
between loads, I almost fall

and it bears me up.
Right then I think:

Wheelbarrow, what if, as the day ends,
when we have dumped the last load,
you spring forward,
carrying me down the dune,
racing your fat wheel
over the vines past the walnut trees,
with me gripping the handles,
my legs flying out behind?
What if you sweep down past the boathouse,
through the marram grass over the sand
out onto the lake toward the setting sun,
skipping over the water like a stone?

III.

The Clarity of a Father's Life

Early on, I envied the clarity of my father's life.
In the Depression,
the only choice was to work harder.
In World War II,
men his age were drafted,
required to serve to the war's end.

He led troops across the Rhine under enemy fire.
He returned a confident Army Major,
a daily communicant at Mass,
a family man, a successful real estate broker,
a community leader.

I couldn't follow his path.
I meant to become a priest
until I felt the Church had failed.
I meant to serve in the Army
until I couldn't support Vietnam.
I did find one good job with one good firm
for all my working life.
I did find one good woman to love,
a spiritual life right for us.
We raised three children
the best we could.

Now I watch our children
on their third and fourth good jobs.
One has suffered divorce.
They raise their children well,
but I think of the joke about modern discipline:

"If I count to 1000 and you're still doing that,
there may be consequences."
They see in me too much structure,
too much work.

As polar ice caps melt,
as African tribes leave ancestral homelands,
migrating over the Sahara to escape drought,
hoping to cross the Mediterranean into Europe,
as the finest nations in the world
build walls against outsiders,
I wonder if our children envy
the clarity of my life.

Parents Know So Little

They first kissed
as actors in a college play.
She soon told us
"He's the one."

They joined an ashram
in Dharamasala,
wrote its monthly letter called
"Seeds of Peace."

They worked an organic farm
in Minnesota.
He showed us proudly
their steaming compost heap
and three small trout
in a nearby stream;
she showed us her recipe cards
she used to sell their vegetables
at the farmers' market.

They married
in a Quaker ceremony.
Melting snow dripped
through the church's stained glass roof
while friends and family
witnessed their love
as the spirit moved, and
signed their wedding parchment.

They adopted their first daughter
from a Chinese orphanage, tearful

for all the other girls they could not take,
returning for a second daughter
as soon as the SARS ban lifted.
They celebrated "gotcha days."

Teaching middle school,
she put him through a PhD,
taking little time off
for her breast cancer,
choosing the harshest treatments
so she could live to see
her daughters' weddings.
He is poised for his career.

Now she tells us
they are separating.
Each has a therapist.
He says they found each other
through their weaknesses,
says she enables their daughter's problems.
She says he has always been
passive-aggressive.
Both say they have been
starved of affection for years.

We help her find a divorce lawyer,
take the girls to the country
for a long weekend,
wonder what they will do
with their Quaker wedding parchment.

Lament for a Son-in-Law

We were delighted
our daughter chose him.
He seemed smart and resourceful,
balanced and real.
For nearly 20 years,
he loved our daughter
and we all loved him.

I especially loved him.
I introduced him to birds.
We spent one rainy night
hunting for mating woodcocks,
hoping to throw ourselves
on our backs under a descending male,
spiral diving from 200 feet high
to brake 2 feet from earth
and present his puffed chest
to his female intended.

I introduced him to fishing.
We spent weekends
casting for King Salmon on the Pere Marquette.
He kept up with a hooked salmon
running downstream with a sideways hop
he'd learned as a high school wrestler.
He fished constantly.
For presents he bought me
my best bonefish gear.

He thanked me for helping
with their daughters' education.

We never had a cross word.

Now, after twenty years of marriage,
he marches toward a divorce
our daughter tried her best to avoid.
One of their adopted Chinese daughters
wants only her mother.
The other wants to be
a social scientist like him.
I read proposed custody agreements
where parents decide
whether to transfer the kids
on Christmas afternoon at 2 or 4 PM.
There seems to be no other woman,
just weekly poker games
and nights at south side jazz clubs
with his fellow teachers.
In nine months he'll be gone,
apparently without a backward glance
at her or at us.

He always seemed to love
our island home in Hope Town.
What do I do now
with the lure he saved after catching
a fat mangrove snapper near Johnny's Cay,
or with this wooden shredding bench he built
for scraping the meat from coconuts
which I found in the pantry and hold in my hands.

My Daughter's Roses

She said she's been too distracted
to tend her roses,
so I stop at her garden in the early morning.

She has seen such sorrows,
each one worse than any
in my lucky life.

Now her older daughter
declines her college scholarship,
quits school.

As usual,
my daughter shares nothing,
goes it alone.

Her roses are overgrown
with sucker silver maples.
I cut each sucker at its base,
toothbrush weed killer
on each open stalk,
feed and water
each spindly rose.

I am no gardener,
but I've tried.
The sun not yet hot,
I leave for work
unaccountably happy.

The Launch

Our daughter declines our dinner invitation,
exhausted from her five-hour drive
back from a college visit to Oberlin.
Our granddaughter accepts,
tells us her mother
has taken her to visit fourteen colleges.
She didn't like the first few,
but she did like Oberlin
after her student guide told her
she didn't need to dress grungy.
She said she's looking forward
to her new SAT scores
after the tutoring her mom arranged,
then to her college acceptances.
She thinks if her mom can teach her to dance,
Prom will be even better than Homecoming.

Next weekend we fish for King Salmon
running to spawn on the Pere Marquette River.
Each female chooses a gravel bed,
pours her eggs down in a milky stream,
and flails the bed with her tail
until the eggs settle underneath,
safe from predator trout.
Her tail turns white
as she beats off its scales on the rocks.
Then without a backward glance at the males
fighting each other in a line behind her,
vying to fertilize her eggs,
she swims off to die.

Berkeley to Chicago

After twelve dry, sunny years in Berkeley,
our son John with his wife Molly and three daughters
will move back this summer
to his hometown of Chicago for a trial year.
Four brave women.
We are overjoyed.

On a snowy Friday night
with the polar vortex closing in,
I mount the steps
of our Michigan cottage,
grab the handrail
through inches of fluffy snow.
The Inuit would call this *aqilokoq*,
softly falling snow.
I hope the four brave women
like *aqilokoq*.

On Saturday, thicker snow
caps the birdfeeders,
bends the boughs
of the Douglas firs.
The Inuit would call this *piegnartoq*,
snow good for driving sleds.
I remember from childhood racing our sleds
down the banks of the Des Plaines River,
returning home with chattering teeth
to a crackling fire and my mother's hot chocolate.
I hope the four brave women
like *piegnartoq*.

On Sunday the snow bites my cheeks.
The Inuit would call this
pukak, the crystalline powder snow
that looks like salt.
Lake Michigan is white to the horizon
with *siguliaksraq*, the patchwork of crystals
that form as the sea begins to freeze.
I remember my mother
bribing me to find my face mask
and hockey skates
and trudge to Fox Park
to skate for two hours.
I resolve to collect a kitty for such days.
I hope the four brave women
can stand *pukak* and *siguliaksraq*.

For Maya at Two

You can't yet
say "grandpop,"
so you call me "Beepop."

At our place
in the Michigan dunes,
I say "Here we go."
You say "Here we go."
We chase ring-billed gulls
off the beach into flight,
water the Knockout Roses,
lop dead branches
from the sugar maple,
watch the house wren
guard its babies
in the birdhouse
by pecking a blue jay
ten times its size.

I give you a sleigh ride
on the sand in the kayak.
I tell you a story
about a raccoon,
and you say "raccoon"
so many times
that we choose some bait
and I tell you I'll catch one
in a Have-a-Heart trap,
so you can see its masked face,
its ringed tail.

I watch you
blow soap bubbles,
putting the wand
into your mouth so often
that you breathe bubbles.

At night
I tell you the story of Maya
and her exciting day.
You lean your blonde head
against my chest.
I sing you
the Paul Robeson spirituals
I sang your father,
until you fall asleep.

Maya at Age Three:
Her Mother Puts Her to Bed

"We need to start going to bed."

"I don't want to go to bed."

"You know what we do:
story, brush teeth, snuggles."

"But first I need to put my babies
to bed with a story."

"It sounds as though
that will take a long time.
Shall I set the timer for three minutes?"

"I don't like the timer."

"I can use my watch instead.
Would you like three or five or four minutes?"

"I don't like those minutes.
I want seven or ten minutes,
or nine or eight minutes."

"Well, I can give you a one-minute warning."

"I need you to help me put my babies to bed.
And I don't want a one-minute warning.
I need a two-minute warning."

"Okay, let's go."

Anna at Two

We walk out on the Berkeley pier
into the San Francisco Bay,
the sun setting over Mount Tam.
Anna is already shrieking
with joy at the wind-beaten waves.
When her father jokes that
she should use her outside voice,
she yells still louder,
running past the spin fishermen,
their heavy sinkers,
their bright lures,
their girlfriends in stiletto heels.
She hectors a herring gull
half her size
until it drops from its perch
on a light post,
catches the air with its wings,
swoops off for a quieter place.

Oh Yes I Will

Our four-year-old granddaughter Anna
loves to disobey so much
that when you tell her
"Do not put your toys away in that box,"
with a defiant glance, she does just that.

I would think of this
as an accident
of her perfect age,
except that my mother
would often say
"You tend to your end,
and I'll tend to mine."
In her later years,
the only way
we could persuade her to do something
was to suggest she do the opposite.

Except that my Irish ancestors
would often work
opposite ends of their farm for days
until they could stand
to talk to each other again.

Family Christmas Visit

I pick up my eight-month-old granddaughter.
She smiles at me.
I smile at her.
She keeps smiling.
I crook my index finger at her.
She smiles again.

Like the Dalai Lama,
she smiles at everyone.

I was raised Roman Catholic.
I am just waiting
for the inevitable first evidence
of original sin.

Later, I am minding the two-year-old.
Across the room
she climbs up
on the coffee table with the glass top,
begins to dance.
I tell her "Stop, honey, get down.
You'll break the glass and cut your feet."
She keeps dancing.
I retrieve my invariably effective parental glare
and say, "Stop and get down."
She dances, just a little slower.
I dredge up the scowl
reserved for special occasions,
the one that suggests a spanking,
the one my kids said made my eyes bulge out,
the one that never failed.

I say, "Get down now."
She gets down from the table, slowly.
Her look tells me
the issue may be revisited.

Oink's

On a warm summer Saturday night,
I take my granddaughters
Maya, Anna and Hazel,
10, 7, and 4,
for ice cream cones at Oink's.
We park in the space labeled "Pork Rind."
The line is out the door.
When we get in,
we take a number.
Anna asks if they can taste different flavors.
I say one taste because the line is so long.
They disappear into the throng to check flavors.
The girl calls out our number.
I order a chocolate chip cone,
scanning the crowd for the girls.
I get my cone and prepare to pay,
glancing back at the long line.
They reappear just in time.   .

Maya gets mint chip.
Hazel gets strawberry.
Anna asks for a taste of butter pecan.
She tastes, cocks her head,
orders grasshopper pie,
a combination of mint chip, fudge and Oreo cookies.
I eat my chocolate chip scoop in large bites.
They lick their scoops slowly,
lazily catching dribbles down the sides of the cones,
each in a race to finish last.

We walk outside.

Hazel looks up at us.
Her strawberry scoop topples,
splats on the sidewalk.
She bursts out crying.
I tell her no problem.
I carve off the side touching the sidewalk,
place the scoop back on the cone,
offer it to her.
She won't have it.
She keeps crying.

I start again at the back of the line.
She still wants strawberry,
but this time in a bigger waffle cone.
Maya and Anna are nearly finished
despite their best efforts to linger.
Anna sits on my lap.
One of her last dribbles of grasshopper pie
drips onto my pants.
My scoop of chocolate chip
settles in my stomach.
Maya finishes.
Anna throws away what remains of her cone.
Hazel is still licking her do-over slowly,
looking lovingly at her nearly full
scoop of strawberry.

At last, I suggest
she share bites with her sisters.
She first says no, then relents.
Maya takes a bite.
Anna takes a bite.
The cone splits in Anna's hand.
I hold the cone parts together

to show Hazel she can still eat it.
She won't have it.
She bursts out crying.
I have Maya take bites to persuade her,
ice cream oozing
through the cracked cone over my fingers.
Nothing works.
I glance again at the back of the line.

Then Anna comforts Hazel.
I see my chance.
I throw out the broken cone.
I look for a water fountain
to wash my hands.
There is none.
I hurry the girls into the car,
drive them home
steering the wheel with my palms,
stretching my sticky fingers up to dry.

Valentina, Age Four, Talks to Her Mother at Bedtime

"I'm getting lazy."

"You're already lazy; that's dizzy."

"I'm lazy."

"Oh, monkey, you just ran into the wall, you have to be careful when you're feeling lazy. You're dizzy. Let's go to bed."

"I am not tired a little or a million."

"You are so tired you're dizzy."

"I am not going to be happy if you keep saying that."

"We need to go to bed."

"You are the most disgusting person in this life."

Shelter from Wet Snow

You could have blamed it
on the rugged brownstone façade
of my narrow apartment
where we took shelter from a wet snowstorm
after our lakefront walk.
Or maybe the crackling fire
in the big stone fireplace
where we warmed ourselves
on my Baroque couch.
Surely not on the makeshift galley kitchen
where I later asked you,
"If I should cook a ham for four hours at 300°,
why can't I cook it for just two at 600°?"

You could have blamed it
on the blue corduroy spread
or the curved mahogany bedstead.

But I say it was
that simple black cotton turtleneck
which was all you were wearing with your jeans
when we took off our wet coats and
stashed them on the coat tree at the door.

The Orange Tent

My grandfather kept his old truck
running more than 30 years
until finally its fenders fell off.

Inspired by his example,
I took my shabby orange pup tent camping
for years on our spring whitewater canoe trips
to the Wisconsin Northwoods.
I kept even its original box
until one night to mock me,
after a few drinks around the campfire,
one friend bellyflopped on it
again and again, reducing it to shreds.

Still, we kept using our tent for years
before another friend shamed me
into providing a better one for Ann,
an igloo style pop-up tent
with a double roof to keep the rain away.

Especially in the dark on the first night
after our long drive north,
our orange tent took twice as long to set up
as I pounded in its many bent tent pegs,
but Ann was patient.
Its inner space was large enough
except when it rained.
Its thin nylon roof sagged and became
so saturated that it soaked our joined sleeping bags
by osmosis at even the slightest touch.

So we learned on those nights
to wrap our sleeping bags tight and
sleep without moving
in the center of the tent.
I remember even now
thinking one night,
as a heavy rain drenched the tent,
a strong wind released the sharp smell
of the Northwoods pines,
and I held Ann close and still,
"I've never been happier in my life."

Your Wedding Hat

We are moving again,
now for a place with fewer stairs.
This time we say
your golden straw wedding hat,
split and cracked after forty-three years,
won't make the move.
I look back at our wedding album,
the hat's shimmering brim
framing your smiling face.

I remember your face under other hats.
The broad-brimmed hat you wore
on our honeymoon on the back trails
of Chichen-Itza
as you trudged behind me,
sure we were lost.

My Cardinals baseball cap
you wore flat-brimmed in the bow
of our whitewater canoe,
ready for the rapids.

Always underneath,
that classic face,
those straight black brows,
those laughing eyes.

I'm keeping the wedding hat.

Baseball and Marriage

The pitcher takes the mound.
The catcher squats behind the plate.
The catcher puts his bare fist
down between his legs,
extending fingers to call the pitch.

If the catcher has more experience,
the pitcher seldom shakes off his sign.
If the pitcher has more,
he may shake off each sign
until the catcher calls the pitch he wants.

The pitcher never catches.
The catcher never pitches.
If communication breaks down,
they reset the signs
in a conference on the mound.

In a marriage,
you sometimes pitch,
you sometimes catch.
One minute you have more experience,
the next minute less.
Certain issues always require
a conference on the mound.

Turquoise Shirt, Crossed Hands

She lies here beside me
face down on the bed
in a turquoise cotton shirt,
arms raised,
beautiful hands crossed,
napping already in mid-morning
after musing about her lack of energy.
Her right knee swells
from a meniscus tear she got
doing the Hero's Pose in yoga.
Her left foot aches
from the plantar fasciitis she got
doing a fifty mile Breast Cancer Walk.
Her stomach still rumbles,
from our dinner years ago
at the best restaurant in Fez, Morocco.

But she plays tennis with joy,
won't miss yoga,
plants her favorite annuals each year,
talks to our children until they quit,
even when they wake her at night with their calls,
greets even those she doesn't know
with an intentional and complete smile.

Respect for the Hungry

In the Depression,
no one was building.
My grandfather's brickyard closed.
He looked for work himself.
But on my grandparents' back fence
was drawn a smiling cat, hobos' code
for a kind woman who welcomed strangers.
My grandmother told her children
to serve a hot meal on the family's best china
to anyone who knocked.

Now starving Haitians
speaking only Creole French
boat to the Bahamas seeking work.
One gaunt Haitian man
is painting our house,
sending his pay
back to his wife and four children
in Port au Prince.

My wife feeds him
tea and sandwiches.
She won't eat lunch
at our accustomed place
on the front porch.
Notwithstanding the language barrier,
she thinks it might feel to him
disrespectful not to be asked to join us
but difficult for him
if he were asked.

Years Later

I bring cappuccino
to your bedside table.
You keep sleeping as I shave.
The sky darkens.
Storm clouds sweep across the lake,
whip the oak branches,
splat the first leaves of autumn
against the window.
You stir.

A church lady now,
a therapist to all your friends,
a grammy with a comfortable lap,
checking daily for the red flag
warning of rip tides.

Yet still,
all these years after I first knew you,
bookish and hardworking,
brown eyes flashing,
teasing me so well I thought
you must know me
as well as I know myself,
still that same fire.

Forty Years

For our 40th wedding anniversary,
we take again our honeymoon vacation
in a centuries-old hacienda
near the Mayan ruins of Uxmal.

The stone structures are unchanged.
Massive, stately quadrangles.
Temples are thrust to the sky by staircases.
Each step's riser is higher than its tread is deep,
so from the temple mount
you see no staircase,
only yellow sun in blue sky,
wide green grass below.

Forty years ago,
we climbed the steps Mayan style,
zigzagging surefooted diagonally up and down,
tracing the pattern of the Mayan sacred serpent.

Now, especially in descent,
we use two feet sideways on each step,
body leaning into the stairs,
upper hand poised to grab a higher step
to keep us from hurtling
down the stone edges below.

But still, after all these years,
our weary bodies cup each other at night,
first this way, then that, hers always warmer,
and before that, thank God for me,
her low, liquid voice recounts the day,
her warm brown eyes always ready to laugh.

ABOUT THE AUTHOR

I grew up in Oak Park, Illinois, the oldest of nine. My parents insisted on Catholic schools, and when I graduated from Notre Dame, I accepted a Rhodes Scholarship, contrary to the advice of my Irish grandparents, who thought I shouldn't study in England. After Yale Law School, I joined Mayer Brown LLP and enjoyed a forty-year commercial real estate practice among the Firm's outstanding and generous lawyers. I served for years as head of the real estate group, played third base on the Firm's 16-inch (no mitts) softball team, and enjoyed teaching analytics and writing to the younger real estate lawyers. I became a Board member and then Chair of IES Abroad, a study abroad organization for American college students; LINK Unlimited, a sponsoring/mentoring organization for African-American high school students; and The Arthur J. Schmitt Foundation, which encourages leadership programs in certain Chicago area Catholic high schools and colleges. I also founded and chair Rust Belt Rising, which helps Midwestern Democratic candidates win elections at all levels by focusing on the fundamental issues of working families. My wife and daughter are excellent published poets, and when I joined the Hope Town Writers Circle, I was drawn to writing poetry. These poems are the result. I hope you enjoy them.

This book is set in a Garamond typeface. During the mid-fifteen hundreds, Claude Garamond — a Parisian punch-cutter — produced a refined array of book types that combined an unprecedented degree of balance and elegance, for centuries standing as the pinnacle of beauty and practicality in type-founding.

For more concerning the work of John Gearen, visit
www.antrimhousebooks.com/authors.html.

This book will be available at all bookstores
including Amazon early in 2021
or you can order immediately
from the author:

John Gearen
721 Ontario St., Apt. 206
Oak Park, IL 60302
jgearen@mayerbrown.com.
Send $20 per book
(checks payable to John Gearen)
plus $3 for shipping.